W0114678

# THE
# GRIFFIN
## AND THE
# DINOSAUR

### HOW ADRIENNE MAYOR
### DISCOVERED A FASCINATING LINK
### BETWEEN MYTH
### AND SCIENCE

**MARC ARONSON** WITH **ADRIENNE MAYOR**
ILLUSTRATED BY **CHRIS MULLER**

NATIONAL
GEOGRAPHIC

WASHINGTON, D.C.

For my brother, Mark Mayor. —A.M.

To John W. Glenn, who keeps our eyes on the prize. —M.A.

Copyright © 2014 Adrienne Mayor and Aronson & Glenn LLC
All rights reserved. Reproduction of the whole or any part of the contents without written permission from the publisher is prohibited.

A Book by Aronson & Glenn LLC
Produced by Marc Aronson and John W. Glenn
Book design and production by Jon Glick, mouse+tiger • Photo and permissions research by Sarah Parvis • Additional research by Susan Bartle, Karen Beimel, Sharon Brinkman, and Shannon Wright

**Published by the National Geographic Society**
John M. Fahey, *Chairman of the Board and Chief Executive Officer*
Declan Moore, *Executive Vice President; President, Publishing and Travel*
Melina Gerosa Bellows, *Executive Vice President; Chief Creative Officer, Books, Kids, and Family*

**Prepared by the Book Division**
Hector Sierra, *Senior Vice President and General Manager*
Nancy Laties Feresten, *Senior Vice President, Kids Publishing and Media*
Jay Sumner, *Director of Photography, Children's Publishing*
Jennifer Emmett, *Vice President, Editorial Director, Children's Books*
Eva Absher-Schantz, *Design Director, Kids Publishing and Media*
R. Gary Colbert, *Production Director*
Jennifer A. Thornton, *Director of Managing Editorial*

**Staff for This Book**
Jennifer Emmett, *Project Editor*
James Hiscott, Jr., *Art Director*
Lori Epstein, *Senior Photo Editor*
Ariane Szu-Tu, *Editorial Assistant*
Callie Broaddus, *Design Production Assistant*
Margaret Leist, *Photo Assistant*
Carl Mehler, *Director of Maps*
Grace Hill, *Associate Managing Editor*
Joan Gossett, *Production Editor*
Lewis R. Bassford, *Production Manager*
Susan Borke, *Legal and Business Affairs*
Cathleen Carey and Moriah Petty, *Interns*

**Manufacturing and Quality Management**
Phillip L. Schlosser, *Senior Vice President*
Chris Brown, *Vice President, NG Book Manufacturing*
George Bounelis, *Vice President, Production Services*
Nicole Elliott, *Manager*
Rachel Faulise, *Manager*
Robert L. Barr, *Manager*

**Photography and Illustration Credits**
Abbreviations: t=top, b=bottom, l=left, r=right
Illustrations on front and back covers and pages 6, 10, 14, 18, 22–23, 26, 28 (photo illustration), 32, 34–35, 36, and 40 by Chris Muller
Decorative illustrations throughout by Jon Glick, adapted from artwork by Adrienne Mayor

Page 7 (inset): courtesy Adrienne Mayor • pages 8–9 (all): courtesy Adrienne Mayor • page 11 (inset): courtesy Adrienne Mayor • page 12: American School of Classical Studies at Athens, Archives in the Blegen Library • page 13 (t): American Numismatic Society • page 13 (b): courtesy Adrienne Mayor • page 15 (inset): courtesy Adrienne Mayor • page 16 (t): pair of griffin protomes, Greek, probably from Samos, Orientalizing Period, late 7th–early 6th century B.C., bronze with bone or ivory inlay, 1: 20.3 x 7.6 x 7.6 cm (8 x 3 x 3 in.); 2: 21.6 x 8.3 x 7 cm (8½ x 3¼ x 2¾ in.), Katherine K. Adler Memorial Fund, 1994.38.1-2, The Art Institute of Chicago, Photography © The Art Institute of Chicago • pages 16 (b) and 17 (all): courtesy Adrienne Mayor • page 19 (inset): head of Polyphemos, late Hellenistic or Roman Period, ca 150 B.C., made in Italy (Dolomitic marble from Thasos), Greek (2nd century B.C.)/Museum of Fine Arts, Boston, Massachusetts, USA/gift in honor of Edward W. Forbes from his friends/The Bridgeman Art Library • page 20 (t): courtesy Adrienne Mayor • page 20 (b): griffins attacking a horse (gold) (detail of 343656 and 343171), Greek School (4th century B.C.)/Historical Museum, Kiev, Ukraine/Photo © Boltin Picture Library/The Bridgeman Art Library • page 24 (all): courtesy Adrienne Mayor • page 25: Universal Images Group/SuperStock • page 27 (inset): plaque in the form of a Scythian horseman brandishing a spear/Werner Forman Archive/The Bridgeman Art Library • page 29: © Ken Backer, Dreamstime.com • pages 30–31: DeAgostini/SuperStock • page 31 (map): illustration by Jon Glick, from map created by Adrienne Mayor • page 33 (inset): Photri Inc./age fotostock/SuperStock • page 37 (inset): © RMN-Grand Palais/Art Resource, NY • pages 38–39: Nimatallah/Art Resource, NY • page 41 (inset): courtesy Adrienne Mayor • page 42: © Bill Brooks/Alamy • page 43 (all): courtesy Adrienne Mayor

**NOTE ABOUT DESIGN AND ILLUSTRATION**

The decorative flourishes throughout the book featuring griffins were adapted by designer Jon Glick from illustrations, prints, and sketches made by Adrienne Mayor.

The paintings opening each chapter were created by artist Chris Muller combining traditional media—pencil and watercolor—and digital painting.

The text for this book was set in Egyptienne F, the captions in Frutiger, and the display type in Galahad and Dear Sarah.

The National Geographic Society is one of the world's largest nonprofit scientific and educational organizations. Founded in 1888 to "increase and diffuse geographic knowledge," the Society's mission is to inspire people to care about the planet. It reaches more than 400 million people worldwide each month through its official journal, *National Geographic*, and other magazines; National Geographic Channel; television documentaries; music; radio; films; books; DVDs; maps; exhibitions; live events; school publishing programs; interactive media; and merchandise. National Geographic has funded more than 10,000 scientific research, conservation and exploration projects and supports an education program promoting geographic literacy.

For more information, please visit www.nationalgeographic.com, call 1-800-NGS LINE (647-5463), or write to the following address:
National Geographic Society
1145 17th Street N.W.
Washington, D.C. 20036-4688 U.S.A.

Visit us online at nationalgeographic.com/books

For librarians and teachers: ngchildrensbooks.org

More for kids from National Geographic:
kids.nationalgeographic.com

For information about special discounts for bulk purchases, please contact National Geographic Books Special Sales: ngspecsales@ngs.org

For rights or permissions inquiries, please contact National Geographic Books Subsidiary Rights: ngbookrights@ngs.org

ISBN: 978-1-4263-1108-6 (Trade hardcover)
ISBN: 978-1-4263-1109-3 (Reinforced library binding)

Printed in Hong Kong
13/THK/1

# CONTENTS

*Chapter One*

# PRAIRIE GIRL

ADRIENNE MAYOR GREW UP IN SIOUX FALLS, South Dakota, where the land stretches from one edge of the sky to another. Some people don't enjoy gazing at mile after mile of corn. They get nervous when the wind makes waves and swells in an ocean of tall grass. Not Adrienne. She loved to walk across the endless flat prairie imagining what it was like for the first people who lived on the plains and dreaming up stories about the animals, plants, rocks, and bugs around her. As Adrienne walked, and looked, and imagined, she was following in the footsteps of her great-grandfather, George Halleck Center.

George was the kind of larger-than-life person you usually only read about in novels. He was born in 1855 in Ohio, and when he was three years old, his family went west in a covered wagon. They settled near St. Louis, where his father ran an amusement park. The famous lawman Wild Bill Hickok enjoyed visiting the park, and soon George was growing his hair as long as Wild Bill's. As a young man, he fell in love with Josephine Eubanks, who was part Native American. George taught Josie to read and write, and she taught him her family's traditional recipes, which he used to make patent medicines. Together they set off around the Midwest in a wagon, accompanied by Sioux dancers who performed to drum up customers.

**Adrienne at six years old, missing a tooth (INSET).**

**A day on the prairie as Adrienne might have experienced it (OPPOSITE).**

7

# G. H. CENTER'S BIG INDIAN SHOW!

IS NOW IN TOWN WITH A BAND OF

## Genuine Sioux Indians.

### WHITE CLOUD

The Chief, is a nephew of the famous Chief Sitting Bull.

### Black Badger, Little Mink, Twenty Rabbits,

### White Bear and Spotted Fawn,

THE QUEEN OF THE NATION.

Giving an exhibition of Indian life, such as you seldom see.

### War, Snake and Green Corn Dances, Scalp

### BEAR AND BUFFALO DANCES,

And showing how their doctors doctor the sick.

RELIGIOUS & MARRIAGE C

Four shows a day—10 A. M., 1 P. M. 4.

SSION, - - - - -

George Halleck Center (BOTTOM) and a poster for his traveling show (LEFT).

Adrienne's dad, John, had been brought up by George and Josephine, so there were endless family tales about his long-haired grandfather, and they came with proof. George was fascinated by the natural world, and he collected things: fossil ferns from the coal mines of southern Illinois, where he had started working when he was just nine years old; arrowheads from ploughed fields; a Gila monster he stuffed and preserved; snapping turtles, butterflies, and creatures that had crawled along the earth millions of years ago. Adrienne's dad kept the collection. At night, each strange find brought on a story, and each story had the same lesson: George had no schooling but made himself into a skilled naturalist. Anyone can become an expert. You just have to be patient, observant, and curious.

As Adrienne walked, she loved the feeling of the vast sky above her, but her eyes were fixed on the ground. She was always looking for that one something special that would stand out in a day of happy wandering. She might find a flower that looked different, a caterpillar, an oddly shaped pebble, even a fossil shell. That was her treasure for the day. She was just like her great-grandfather: She had found a wonder. Then as she walked on she made up new stories about her latest discovery. To Adrienne, endless flat land under a big sky meant freedom: She could explore forever, and she could fill her mind with stories.

In school, Adrienne was quiet. She was the shy girl who hardly ever speaks up, never raises her hand or tries to catch the teacher's eye. But shyness was only part of the problem: Adrienne did not like studying what other people thought she needed to know. Instead, she read on her own, poring over the myths and legends of Greece and Rome and other lands. As she read, she drew pictures, illustrating the tales. She even took a military history class just so she could learn about ancient battles. When it seemed like the teacher droned

on, she faded away—turning more interesting stories over in her mind.

Adrienne went off to college in Minnesota—where far too many trees blocked the sky—worked in the post office, and studied printmaking. In a way, she was going on another long walk: searching for a question that would be so important to her, she would study it forever. She had no way of knowing that the clue she needed was waiting thousands of miles away, in a library in Athens, Greece.

Adrienne makes camp on one of her many travels after she left Minnesota, 1968 (ABOVE).

Adrienne never lost her love of art and printmaking. She made this print of a young Amazon and a griffin during her adventures in Greece (BELOW).

*Chapter Two*

# THE SOUND OF HEAT

**W**HEN THE TEMPERATURE GETS HIGH enough in midsummer, cicadas make a strange, loud noise that is something like a cross between a rattle and a crashing wave. When Adrienne first heard the cicadas, they sounded to her like outer space music, or the engines of a giant UFO. She was sitting in the library of the American School of Classical Studies in Athens, while cicadas and doves filled the fig trees outside the windows. The buzz of the insects made the air shimmer, as if they were turning the relentless heat into sound.

There was no air-conditioning. Overhead fans turned on their slow, endless round doing nothing for the four scholars seated at the wooden table beneath them. Despite the heat and the insect symphony, Adrienne was in heaven. While Josiah (Josh) Ober, her fiancé, worked on his research into ancient Greek fortresses and democracy,

Adrienne was free to wander in new fields: the pages of ancient Greek literature. But she was no mere tourist. She was a hunter, out searching for prey.

No one could have been more of an outsider in that library than Adrienne. She was sitting next to experts in the classics. Each one had spent years, decades even, focusing ever

**Adrienne sketches at an ancient Greek fortress, ca 1978–79 (INSET).**

**This modern painting of an Amazon fighting a griffin echoes the colors and images that Adrienne found so fascinating in ancient Greek sources (OPPOSITE).**

more narrowly on his or her own special field of study. One might have spent a lifetime studying the surviving scraps and fragments of a single ancient writer. Another had tracked down every surviving mention of a particular goddess. A third had explored temple ruins in some remote corner of the country and could describe each stone he'd seen. It had taken Adrienne ten years to earn her college degree. She saw herself as an artist like her mother, certainly not a scholar.

Still, Adrienne was that girl who loved nature and knew how to spin a story from a strange find. She understood how you see—what you notice—when you scan the ground and watch the sky as carefully as the experts around her examined their books and stones. And as she read through her own stack of books filled with ancient tales, she

Adrienne spent much of her time in Athens in this room of the Blegen Library at the American School of Classical Studies (ABOVE). Four or five scholars would share a table with Adrienne, each marking their tabletop turf with piles of books. This photo was taken in 1912, and Adrienne says the library had hardly changed when she studied there 70 years later!

saw something familiar: When the ancient Greeks described some legendary creatures, especially the hybrid of a lion and an eagle they called a "griffin," they sounded like people talking about a real animal they had actually observed. Adrienne, who grew up hearing about the quirky discoveries of George Halleck Center, recognized her own way of seeing and thinking in those ancient words. But what creature with four legs and a beak like a bird could have been so real to the Greeks thousands of years ago? Nothing still living, of course, but—remembering her great-grandfather's collection of curiosities—she asked herself, "What kind of bones, what sorts of fossils, might have inspired them?"

One day Adrienne got the clue that she was looking for. The ancient Greeks had come across bones eroding out of the ground on the island of Samos. Indeed, modern Greek farmers were still finding fossils in their fields. Could what the islanders called the "monster of Samos" have been the source of the griffin legend? She rushed off to Samos to find out.

A Greek coin, ca 490 B.C., shows a cicada and a griffin (RIGHT). Many coins featured griffins because the Greeks believed griffins were guardians of treasure.

Josh and Adrienne overlooking the ancient "Road of the Towers" in Greece, 1979 (BELOW).

*Chapter Three*

# SKETCHING GRIFFINS

**A**DRIENNE STEAMED INTO SAMOS EXPECTING to dash right up to the local post office, where the huge fossil bones were stored. When her boat landed, though, she was greeted with a wonderful surprise. The island housed a small archaeological museum, and it was filled with hundreds of bronze griffins. In ancient times, Samos had been a center of worship for the goddess Hera, Zeus's wife, and craftsmen had cast many bronze griffins in her honor. Adrienne took out her notebook and began drawing the griffins. She soon noticed that the more ancient the bronzes, the more they resembled something fierce, predatory, and prehistoric.

Surely the first artists had been looking at the very bones she was about to see in the dusty post office. Then later, over time, the image of the griffin shifted away from fossils to legend. In one trip, Adrienne's hunch would be proven. All she had to do was find the post office, convince the mayor of the town to give her the key to the storeroom, and see the griffin face-to-face.

Or so she thought.

When the key turned in the lock Adrienne saw the bones of . . . the prehistoric ancestor

**Adrienne on her first ferry trip to Samos, 1978 (INSET).**

**Bronze cauldrons decorated with griffin heads filled the great temple of Samos as offerings to the goddess Hera (OPPOSITE).**

A pair of griffin protomes, probably from the Greek island of Samos, and dating to the late 7th–early 6th century B.C. (RIGHT). A protome is a decoration often found on ancient bronze cauldrons.

Adrienne took these photos of the griffins she saw in Samos (BELOW). Her sketches and notes were a way to pay attention to the various details that the ancient Greeks illustrated (OPPOSITE).

of the giraffe. They were huge, impressive, weird—and nothing at all like the griffins. These fossils could never have led the bronze casters to craft the griffin heads she had just seen.

When animals in the wild are hungry, they have a clear picture of what they want to catch. Scientists call this a "search image"—the picture a predator has in its mind that allows it to shut out distractions and zoom toward supper. Scientists looking for fossils use the same language—as they walk about in nature they cannot look at everything. Instead, they begin with a mental picture of what they hope, or expect, to find. This makes for faster, more efficient bone hunting. But it can

top photos view of 3 v. primitives & cast early w/ vestigial knobs — sm ears — ‹crown — protruding eyes — 2 knobs — (beak maybe not so long) — front

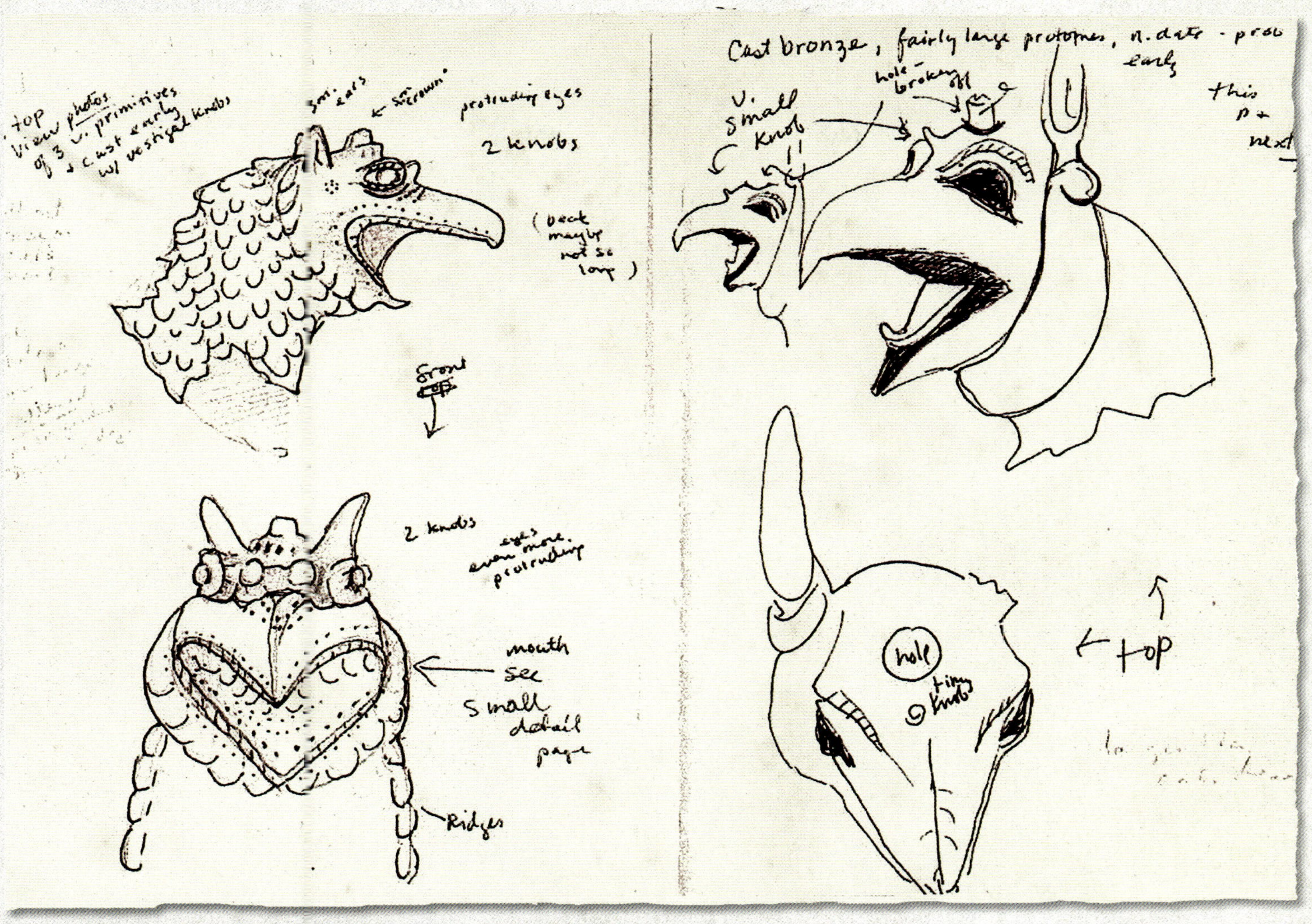

Cast bronze, fairly large protomes, n. date - prob early — v. small knob — hole broken off — this p + next

2 knobs — eyes even more protruding — mouth see small detail page — Ridges

hole — tiny knobs — top

also serve as a blind—preventing the experts from seeing what is right in front of their noses.

Adrienne left Samos with a sketchbook full of diverse griffins, and a lesson. The Greeks were always finding fossil bones, but that does not mean they were always finding griffins. She would have to go back to her books in the heat of the library, to see who first mentioned griffins and where they said the animals lived. For the first time, but certainly not the last, she would have to refine her search image.

*Chapter Four*

# THE CYCLOPS AND THE GRIFFIN PUP

ADRIENNE AND JOSH SPENT ALL OF 1978 in Greece and came back for part of every year thereafter for a decade. Those ten summers gave Adrienne just about all the time she needed. For the lesson of Samos was that she was going to have to turn herself into an expert. She could not dash off to random sites in Greece where large bones had been discovered. Instead she would need to read through every surviving ancient account in Greek and Latin that she could find, to trace how the story of the griffin grew and changed. Who first mentioned them? Where were they supposed to be? What did they look like?

Today searches like that can be done on computers. Many ancient texts have been converted into digital files whose treasures can be found by anyone who knows the great secret of digital research: Computers are very fast and very dumb. They quickly bring you precisely what you asked them to get, not what you meant them to find. During Adrienne's decade under the swirling fans, no one in the library used a computer, and none of the texts were online. Indeed, many of the terms she was looking for were not even listed in the existing indexes. She had become a historical detective.

**An ancient sculpture of the head of a Cyclops, ca 150 B.C. (INSET).**

**The Roman author Aelian believed that gold-hunting nomads snuck past griffins at night to steal their gold (OPPOSITE).**

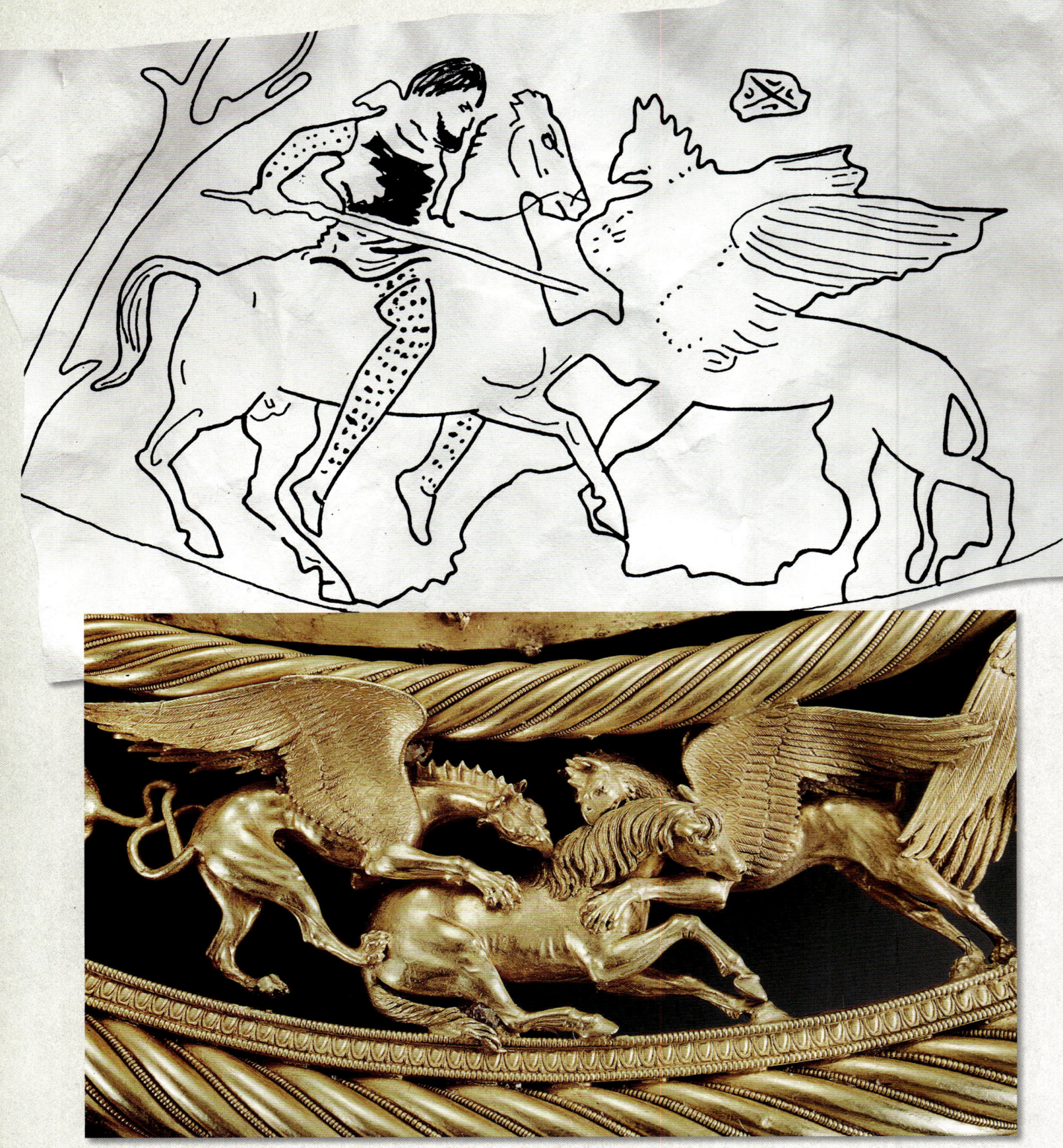

Griffins attack a horse in this detail from a large gold pectoral, a Scythian ornament worn on the chest, ca 4th century B.C. (ABOVE).

FIRST CLUE: Back in the 1820s a geologist traveling in Siberia listened carefully to the local legends and stories. He learned that people often found the giant bones of creatures they called "bird-monsters." Could these fossils of long-extinct rhinos and mammoths have been the source of the griffin legend? How? The bones were north of the Arctic Circle, thousands upon thousands of miles from Greece, and they did not resemble griffins in the slightest. Adrienne's hunch that the ancient griffin was based on fossils came from her own experience as a child—people who pay close attention to nature often ground their stories in what they can actually see and touch. She needed to find bones that any normal person could notice and visualize as belonging to a strange bird with four legs.

In Samos Adrienne found a trove of griffin figures and local fossils, but they did not match. In the record of the traveling geologist, she found a link between fossils and bird-monster legends, but in the wrong place with the wrong bones. Where could she turn? To her books. Then, to the learned scholars studying next to her beneath the fans.

SECOND CLUE: Reading through the classics looking for monster myths and reports of giant bones, Adrienne soon discovered that she was not the first to make the general connection. Other scholars had noticed how often Greeks reported finding giant, unusual, or ancient bones and then displayed them in temples. The Greeks identified the immense bones as the remains of giants, monsters, or mythic heroes. But for hundreds of years modern experts had insisted that creatures such as griffins were the product of fantasy and superstition. Indeed, one scholar made the extremely strange claim that the fossil bones were so big that people long ago would not have noticed them. And yet there were the oddballs, the outsiders, who disagreed.

A Scythian horseman battles a griffin in a sketch that Adrienne made of a scene on an ancient vase (OPPOSITE TOP). She was fascinated by the gold nugget above the griffin and also by how the griffin seems to be rising out of the desert-like scenery.

One of these dissenters was an Austrian paleontologist named Othenio Abel. Back in 1914, Dr. Abel had been exploring fossil sites throughout Europe and Greece. Some of these were in caves among the many islands of the Aegean Sea. As he examined the bones he was finding, he linked them to one of the most famous of mythological creatures: the Cyclops. The one-eyed, man-eating ogre was said to dwell in a cave where he dined on shipwrecked sailors, scattering their bones around his lair. In caves on the coasts of Aegean islands, Abel frequently found the skulls of prehistoric ancestors of the elephant. The Cyclops was not a fantasy. Ancient Greek sailors found what looked liked one-eyed skulls surrounded by bones, and made a reasonable effort to

**MAMMOTH**

explain what they saw. Dr. Abel's theory did not convince everyone—but when Adrienne found it, she was encouraged. The link between fossil and myth was there, if you just looked carefully enough.

**THIRD CLUE:** In the 1980s the American School was still a formal place where work came to a stop promptly at four in the afternoon. Then, prim women in starched uniforms would serve tea to the scholars. Every day as the clock edged closer to teatime, Adrienne rehearsed her speech and mustered up her courage. For during the break she would have her one chance to speak with the venerable archaeologist Dr. Judith Binder. Dr. Binder was a legend in her own right—she was said to have saved the treasures of Athens from the Nazis 40 years earlier, during World War II.

**CYCLOPS**

A sketch (ABOVE RIGHT) of the bronze relief (ABOVE LEFT), ca 630 B.C., showing a griffin mother with her pup that Adrienne was excited to see on her trip to the museum in Olympia.

She had remained in Athens, a guardian of scholarship and tradition, ever since. You had one moment with her, and you needed to present yourself perfectly or she would dismiss you. Finally, Adrienne approached the great lady and told her about her quest to find the source of the griffin. "You must go to Olympia," the formidable scholar replied, "to see the griffin pup."

Of course the archaeologist was right. For in the museum at the ancient home of the Olympic Games, Adrienne found a bronze sculpture of a griffin mother hovering over her young. Outside of one image of the baby Minotaur with his puzzled, distressed human mother, Greek artists never showed mythical creatures as babies or with their parents. Whoever created this naturalistic

scene in about 630 B.C. seemed to be illustrating something real, not just a fantasy.

**THE TRAIL OF CLUES:** Summer after summer, Adrienne combed through the ancient writings and began to put together the pieces of the puzzle. The first griffin stories were not set on Samos, not in Greece at all. Starting in about 675 B.C., Greek writers reported that griffins guarded gold in Scythia.

Here is one example of a clue Adrienne found in an ancient text: Aelian was a Roman who lived several centuries after the ancient Greeks first mentioned griffins. But he spoke and read excellent Greek and gathered together stories about nature and the world from earlier sources. Aelian wrote, "People say that the griffin has four legs and is about the size of a lion, with strong claws and a head with a beak, like an eagle. These griffins make their nests on the ground."

"The gold hunters of Scythia," he explained, "claim that griffins guard the precious metal." But Aelian was not convinced—he guessed that when the humans approach, "the griffins fear for their young, and so give battle to

Scythian warriors adorn a gold comb, ca 5th–3rd century B.C. (ABOVE).

the intruders." Still the animals are fearsome and dangerous, so the hunters sneak up "at night when they are less likely to be detected. Now, the place where the griffins live and the gold is found is a grim and terrible desert. Waiting for a moonless night, the treasure seekers come with shovels and sacks and dig. If they manage to elude the griffins, the men reap a double reward, for they escape with their lives and bring home a cargo of gold."

## Chapter Five

# NOMADS AND GOLD

**T**HE SCYTHIANS DO NOT MAKE IT into most textbooks. They did not develop a written language, so their history is recorded only by visitors and enemies, or in silent archaeological sites. And yet, there is something really interesting about the mysterious horse riders who drank from gold-covered human skulls. The Scythians were a network of related tribes stretching from the Black Sea all the way to Mongolia. They were herders, gold prospectors, and traders. Indeed, for some 800 years, starting in about 700 B.C., trade with nomadic Scythians linked Greece with the exotic, little-known lands of Central Asia and China. Their long-distance migration routes later became the fabled Silk Road.

Fierce fighters, the Scythians dipped their arrows in snake venom and were such skilled archers that they practiced shooting at sparkling gems embedded in distant cliffs. Expert equestrians, they spent most of their lives on horseback and were buried with their steeds, weapons, and gold. These elusive nomads remained unconquered by the ancient world's greatest commanders, including Alexander the Great.

The cold of Siberia has preserved the bodies of Scythian warriors, male and female, buried in graves. For in Scythia, women were free to ride, hunt, and go into battle

**Gold plaque of a Scythian horseman, ca 4th century B.C. (INSET).**

**Modern drawing of a gold Scythian griffin head, ca 7th century B.C. (OPPOSITE).**

This photo illustration replicates the griffin tattoo found on the mummified remains of a Scythian chieftain, ca 5th century B.C. (ABOVE).

beside the men. Their bodies are tattooed with fantastic animals including griffins.

The Scythians were famous for their golden treasures, and wore golden armor in battle. Marvelous hoards of Scythian gold jewelry, cups, and armor have been found in burial mounds in Ukraine, Russia, and Kazakhstan. But their goldfields were secret, known only to nomadic prospectors.

The nomads' gold-hunting region was so poorly mapped that even when Adrienne looked for it in a modern atlas, she found that the publishers had dumped it into the middle of the pages, tucked into the book binding, where you could not make any sense of the map. Yet the Greek sources agreed: Scythian nomads knew where to find gold—in a barren desert guarded by griffins. If she could figure out where the Scythians got their gold, she would know where to look for the fossil bones of the "bird-monster."

When Adrienne and Josh were not tramping around Greece looking for ancient roads and fortresses, they lived in Bozeman, Montana, where Josh taught at Montana State University and Adrienne worked as an artist and editor. For Adrienne, this was a wonderful stroke of luck and the scene of an embarrassing disaster. First the disaster: In 1983, Jack Horner, the most famous (and self-taught) dinosaur hunter in America, became the curator of the Museum of the Rockies at MSU. Adrienne had a question for him. Even as she was hunting for the sources of Scythian gold, she thought she had found a dinosaur that perfectly matched the description of the griffin: the *Triceratops*. Having found the courage to speak to Dr. Binder and other great scholars in Athens, she was willing to brave entering

Horner's office at MSU. But after he answered her question, she left as quickly as she could.

Jack Horner had tartly informed her that the *Triceratops* dinosaur lived only in North America, not Asia. She had made the most rookie mistake—talking about a subject without knowing a thing about it. Adrienne did not even know that certain dinosaurs had lived in specific locations. She assumed all species were scattered

Looking at *Triceratops* fossils such as this (BELOW), Adrienne thought she had found the source of the griffin, until she spoke with Jack Horner.

everywhere. Starting in 1978, she had been reading her way through ancient texts, becoming a kind of stealth classics scholar. Now she would have to start over again, as a self-trained paleontologist. And yet it was not quite as bad as she thought. After Adrienne rushed out of his office, she overheard Horner telling a colleague that "she doesn't know a thing about dinosaurs, but she may be on to something" with her griffin theory.

Next, the stroke of luck: MSU was home not only to Jack Horner, but also to a collection of maps originally made for secret spy agencies and now released to the public. The governments of Russia and China, which now ruled ancient Scythian lands, were as secretive as the Scythians. They did not want anyone to know where they found gold. But the CIA had figured it out. There was gold in a desert region between the Altay Mountains of Mongolia and the Tian Shan range of China. And, as Adrienne knew, there were rich archaeological sites in the same area showing that nomads had gathered gold there thousands of years ago. She had traced the griffin legend from Greece back to Scythia and from the general area to the specific locale where gold hunters had reported seeing the terrifying animals. That left one giant question: Were there any easily visible fossils in those desert sands?

A Scythian scabbard, ca 340–320 B.C. (BELOW). In the triangular panel at top left, a large griffin attacks a deer from left to right. In the main panel at bottom far left, perpendicular to the warriors, two griffins face each other.

# GOLD DEPOSITS AND DINOSAUR FOSSILS IN CENTRAL ASIA

SILK ROAD
DINOSAUR FOSSIL EXPOSURES
GOLD DEPOSITS

● GOLD

Kazakhstan

● GOLD

● GOLD

Mongolia

● GOLD
ALTAY MOUNTAINS

TIAN SHAN

● GOLD

● GOLD

● GOLD

● GOLD

GOBI

● GOLD

● GOLD

TAKLIMAKAN DESERT

● GOLD

● GOLD

● GOLD

● GOLD

● GOLD

China

Adrienne knew she was on the right track when she made a sketch that combined information from CIA maps about gold deposits in Central Asia with known dinosaur fossil exposures (ABOVE). As in Aelian's story (see page 25), the gold was near the griffins.

*Chapter Six*

# THE SECRET OF THE FLAMING CLIFFS

I N THE 1980S THERE WERE NO HANDY databases that could tell Adrienne which skeletons lurked in the dunes and weathered cliffs of the Central Asian deserts. Worse yet, the government of China forbade most foreign scientists from working there. She would have to look through every journal kept by travelers before the strict rules were put into place and make her own catalog of ancient creatures. Every time Adrienne visited a friend at a university, she rushed to the library to seek out information about the fossils of the western Gobi, a desert in Central Asia. And then in the summer of 1986, as she and Josh headed from Bozeman back to Athens, they stopped off to stay with friends in Ithaca, New York—home of Cornell University. Another college, another library: Adrienne was off to the stacks, where she met Indiana Jones.

A reconstructed *Protoceratops* skeleton (INSET).

A skull of the *Proto-ceratops andrewsi*, the dinosaur found by Roy Chapman Andrews in the Gobi (OPPOSITE).

The dashing Indiana Jones, with his whip and leather hat, was based on the real explorer and adventurer Roy Chapman Andrews. Andrews was an American who set out for the Gobi in 1922, looking for what the Chinese called "dragon bones." In the Cornell library Adrienne read through his *On the Trail of Ancient Man*, where he described his journey to the "Flaming Cliffs" of the Gobi. The book is illustrated with original black-and-white photographs of his fossil discoveries, which are now displayed in the American Museum of Natural History in New York. Adrienne turned the pages eagerly, and suddenly found herself face-to-face with an ancient griffin.

*Protoceratops* was a four-legged dinosaur the size of a wolf or a lion, with the shoulder blades of a bird and a large curved beak. And where is this fossil found? Exactly where the Scythians went to hunt for gold. Yet one photo is not enough. What if Andrews had found one rare specimen? That could hardly begin a legend. By now, the Chinese were starting to allow Canadian and American paleontologists to visit the Gobi. Adrienne wrote to two famous experts, Philip Currie and Dale Russell, who had recently been to

the sand dunes. How visible are the fossils, she asked? Could a Scythian gold hunter have seen them? Yes, certainly, came the reply. In fact the *Protoceratops* fossils are so plentiful that there are nests, eggs, even fossil hatchlings in the sand. No wonder the Greeks had sculpted a mother griffin with her "pup"— that is exactly what the nomads must have described.

Adrienne, the girl who walked in fields and made up stories about her discoveries, had been on the right track. The Greeks and Scythians were keen observers of remarkable natural evidence. The Cyclops, griffins, and perhaps even other strange creatures were not fantasies, superstitions, or symbols. They were descriptions based on real, specific fossil bones. The quiet girl gave a voice to the long-silent Scythians. But would anyone listen?

**PROTOCERATOPS**

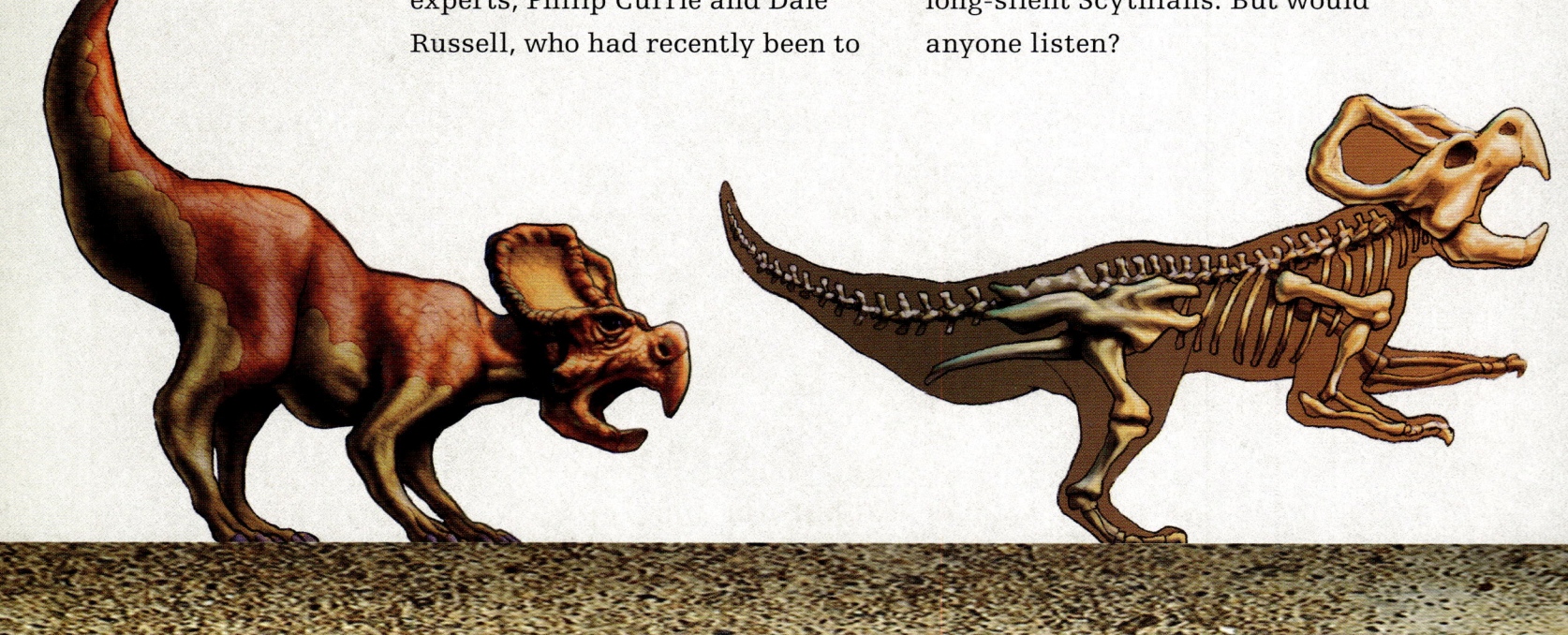

GRIFFIN

*Chapter Seven*

# BATTLEFIELD OF THE GODS

ADRIENNE WAS NOW CERTAIN SHE WAS right, and yet she was a total outsider—she had done all of her research on her own and had no advanced degrees. She still saw herself as an artist, not a writer. But having spent more than a decade in this quest, she could not keep her results to herself. First, she sent her work to a magazine for cryptozoologists—people who hunt for strange new species and possibly legendary creatures, such as the Yeti, the Loch Ness Monster, or the kraken. Though some of the readers of the magazine were believers, ready to trust any report of a new sighting, others were scholars who used it as a way to keep an eye out for interesting discoveries.

The goddess Artemis aims her bow at a giant, in a detail from a painting of the Gigantomachy (War of the Giants), ca 400–390 B.C. (INSET).

Finding bones in the smoldering soil of Megalopolis, ancient Greeks imagined they were seeing the remains of a mythic struggle (OPPOSITE).

Dr. Peter Dodson, the world's leading expert on dinosaurs with beaks, read Adrienne's article. Try as he might, he could not find anything wrong with her theory or her logic, and he said so in print. With that assurance, she sent her theory and

evidence to *Archaeology* magazine, where it would be judged by professionals. They had their doubts—until they read her work. "You've hit it out of the park," an editor assured her. Unfortunately, since Adrienne did not play or watch baseball, she was not sure if that

37

was good or bad. When she saw the published piece, she knew what a home run looked like. That meant she could start her real work.

Adrienne's decade-long quest to prove that the griffin legend was based on a real fossil always had a larger aim. She was certain that the peoples of the ancient world had been as attentive to fossils and bones as we are today. If the Cyclops was an extinct mammoth and the griffin was a *Protoceratops*, surely many other myths and legends were based on observation, not fantasy. Which ones? Adrienne pursued one hot clue in southern Greece, a day's journey from the library in Athens.

If you read Greek myths with your mind on fossils, you immediately notice a promising thread: the Greek belief that the Earth had once been populated by gigantic creatures that no longer existed. According to Greek myth, these giants and monsters, like the Cyclops, Hydra, and Typhon, arose in different ages in the deep past— and they all had been destroyed in a series of wars with Zeus, the other gods, and great heroes like Hercules. These ancient ideas about huge, vanished creatures are similar to our modern sense of different geological ages, some of which featured large creatures such as dinosaurs or mammoths. Could it be that the

Greeks actually saw the bones of monstrous creatures mixed with the bones of what looked like giants? And if they did, would they have had any reason to assume these long-dead enemies met in battle? As Adrienne was discovering, the overwhelming answer to both questions was "Yes!"

"Megalopolis" means "giant city," and that was the name the ancient Greeks gave to a city they built in about 370 B.C. It was located in one of the precise spots where the myths said that Zeus destroyed an army of giants. Why was this place seen as the site of an ancient cosmic war?

One answer started to become clear in 1902, when a local man hunting for a lost axe uncovered giant ivory tusks in the ground. That drew the attention of a paleontologist from Athens, who went on to discover five tons of fossil bones at the site. The ancients had observed and collected large fossilized bones, so they had every reason to believe that many gigantic creatures had died there—but why did they assume the bizarre beings had fought a battle? The ground around the ancient ruins of Megalopolis is mostly lignite, soft peat coal, which can catch fire when it is struck by bolts of lightning and then continues to hiss and smolder endlessly. The myths told how Zeus defeated the giants with shafts of lightning, and the Greeks thought they

Gods battle the giants in a frieze, or sculpted scene, ca 525 B.C. (ABOVE). The giants, shown here in helmets, fight from right to left and the gods from left to right. In the center, the god Apollo and his sister, the goddess Artemis, chase down a fleeing giant.

had the evidence to prove it. There were blackened bones of nightmare creatures in the ground, while the smoking soil still bore the scars of the heavenly fires.

Adrienne continued to search through myths, matching ancient reports of people finding huge bones with local legends and what she now knew about the habitats of extinct creatures that had lived millions of years ago. She had identified the model for the griffin, brought Abel's explanation of the Cyclops back to light, and now was filling in a full map of ancient Greece, highlighting the crossing points of fossil and myth. In 2000, Princeton University Press published her first book, *The First Fossil Hunters: Paleontology in Greek and Roman Times*, and the world took note. Not only had the quiet girl proven her initial hunch, she opened a new door—created a new search image—for scholars everywhere. And that is why her work has only begun.

# Chapter Eight
# STORIES, STORIES, EVERYWHERE

AFTER ADRIENNE'S BOOK CAME OUT and was featured in newspapers, museums began to build exhibits around myths and fossils, TV crews came to film her, and magazine after magazine profiled her. She and Josh settled in at Stanford University, where he is a professor and she is a research scholar in the Classics Department and the History and Philosophy of Science program. Adrienne expanded her search, turning back to her own childhood and the stories of her great-grandfather.

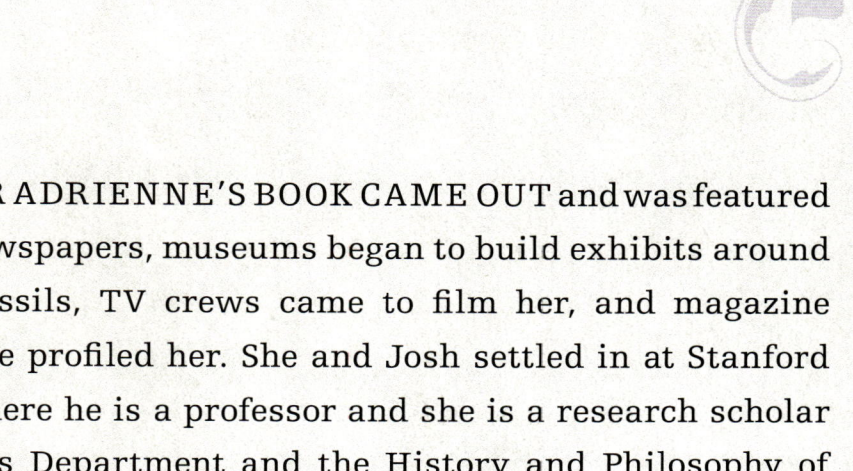

A skull of a mosasaur, a marine reptile from the Cretaceous era, ca 145–65 million years ago (INSET).

Adrienne believes that some Native American legends about water monsters were based on mosasaur fossils they saw (OPPOSITE).

She traveled through the United States, matching Native American stories of the battles of thunderbirds and water monsters with the kinds of fossils Jack Horner, Peter Dodson, and other paleontologists have excavated. Once again, people who lived close to nature have proven to be astute observers who understood that the land they lived on had been through many phases—shells and sea creatures stranded on mountains that had once been under oceans, petrified forests where giant animals with horns had once roamed, hillsides where thunderstorms exposed the immense bones of monsters killed by lightning long ago when the Earth was young.

There is a whole world of myths to explore, and Adrienne has done what she had hoped to do, showing how to link stories and fossils and other mysterious natural evidence. She continues to uncover intriguing grains of truth in myths around the globe. For example, she is studying the realities behind ancient Amazons, fierce warrior women in Greek mythology, inspired by real horsewomen-archers of Scythia. It turns out that those women warriors' graves are filled with weapons and gold exactly where the Greeks said Amazons lived in antiquity. She is also trying to figure out the true identity of the legendary poison that was rumored to have killed Alexander the Great, and she is working with linguists to decipher strange words inscribed on ancient Greek vases. For a paleontological museum exhibit, she worked with an artist who created a fantasy skeleton of a centaur to understand how the Greeks might have visualized it.

So far, Adrienne has consulted with scholars and scientists in Europe, Australia, Russia, China, India, Iran, Turkey, Egypt, Mexico, and South America about connections they are seeing between local myths and fossils. For example, she has collaborated with scholars in India to understand the influence of fossils of bizarre extinct creatures

An ancient Native American rock painting near Lake Superior shows warriors in a canoe with three water monsters (BELOW). Could these creatures be attempts to identify bizarre fossils seen eroding out of lake shores or banks of rivers?

The "Centaur of Tymphi," a fantastic creature created by artist William Willers from human and zebra bones (LEFT).

Adrienne's research has taken her to Vietnam (BELOW TOP) and China (BELOW BOTTOM), where she viewed fossilized dinosaur eggs.

in the foothills of the Himalaya on some of the best known Indian epics, such as the *Mahabharata*. She has co-authored several articles with paleontologists in Canada, Portugal and China about the ancient folklore surrounding dinosaur tracks, to learn how ordinary people in ancient times combined reason and imagination to explain such remarkable footprints in store.

Adrienne Mayor changed the search image for all of us. We were all too ready to believe that only people like us—modern people with computers and smartphones—could possibly have made good sense of the world around them. People of antiquity, our ancestors, must have been irrational, superstitious, blind to the evidence around them. The girl who loved to walk in the cornfields, the great-granddaughter of the self-taught naturalist, knew that this was not true. Once we opened our own eyes to ancient stories and natural evidence, we could marvel at what those who came before us observed, investigated, pondered, and understood. Now, following in their footsteps, we can begin to see the world that they explored, and that we inhabit.

# ADRIENNE'S QUEST FOR THE GRIFFIN

**ARCTIC CIRCLE**

CANADA

NORTH AMERICA

BRITISH COLUMBIA

UNITED KINGDOM

*Adrienne found the government maps at MSU here, which allowed her to learn exactly where the Scythians would have hunted for gold.*

MONTANA
Bozeman

MINN.
Lake Superior

*Site of Stanford University, where Adrienne and Josh now teach.*

SOUTH DAK.
Sioux Falls

N.Y.
Ithaca

New York

*Balearic Islands*
SPAIN

Palo Alto

St. Louis
ILL.    OH.

*Adrienne found the key photo of Protoceratops in a book here.*

MISSOURI

PORTUGAL

UNITED STATES

MEXICO

*Adrienne grew up, went to school, and explored the prairie here.*

*Adrienne's great-great grandfather ran an amusement park here in the 1860s.*

**TROPIC OF CANCER**

*Canary Islands*
SPAIN

*Pacific
Ocean*

*Atlantic
Ocean*

**EQUATOR**

## MAP KEY

Country or state
mentioned in this book

BRAZIL

SCYTHIA

SOUTH
AMERICA

Country where scientists are
consulting with Adrienne and
linking fossils with folklore

**TROPIC OF CAPRICORN**

| 0 | miles | 2,000 |
|---|-------|-------|

| 0 | kilometers | 3,000 |
|---|-----------|-------|

ARGENTINA

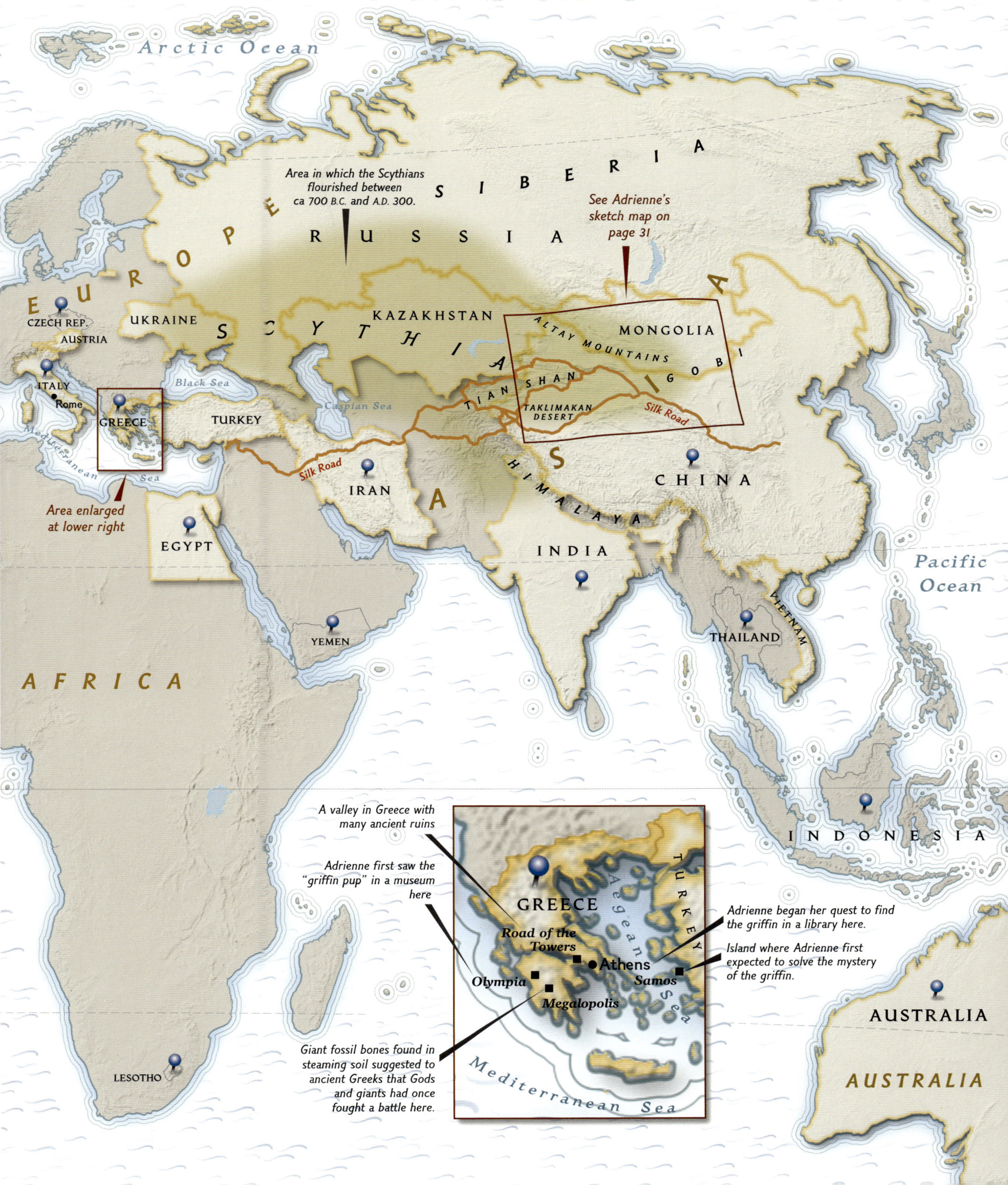

Arctic Ocean

EUROPE

CZECH REP.
AUSTRIA
ITALY
Rome
GREECE

Area enlarged
at lower right

Mediterranean Sea

AFRICA

LESOTHO

RUSSIA

SIBERIA

Area in which the Scythians
flourished between
ca 700 B.C. and A.D. 300.

UKRAINE

SCYTHIA

KAZAKHSTAN

See Adrienne's
sketch map on
page 31

MONGOLIA

ALTAY MOUNTAINS

GOBI

Black Sea

Caspian Sea

TIAN SHAN

TAKLIMAKAN
DESERT

Silk Road

TURKEY

Silk Road

IRAN

A

EGYPT

YEMEN

HIMALAYA

S

INDIA

CHINA

VIETNAM

THAILAND

Pacific
Ocean

INDONESIA

AUSTRALIA

AUSTRALIA

A valley in Greece with
many ancient ruins

Adrienne first saw the
"griffin pup" in a museum
here

Giant fossil bones found in
steaming soil suggested to
ancient Greeks that Gods
and giants had once
fought a battle here.

GREECE

Road of the
Towers

Olympia

Megalopolis

Athens

Aegean Sea

TURKEY

Samos

Adrienne began her quest to find
the griffin in a library here.

Island where Adrienne first
expected to solve the mystery
of the griffin.

Mediterranean Sea

# SUGGESTIONS FOR FURTHER READING

## BOOKS BY ADRIENNE MAYOR

Mayor, Adrienne. *The First Fossil Hunters: Dinosaurs, Mammoths, and Myth in Greek and Roman Times*. Rev. ed. Princeton, NJ: Princeton UP, 2011. First published in 2000 with the title *The First Fossil Hunters: Paleontology in Greek and Roman Times*.

Mayor, Adrienne. *Fossil Legends of the First Americans*. Princeton, NJ: Princeton UP, 2005.

Mayor, Adrienne. *Greek Fire, Poison Arrows, and Scorpion Bombs: Biological and Chemical Warfare in the Ancient World*. Woodstock, NY: Overlook Duckworth, 2003, rev. ed. 2009.

Mayor, Adrienne. *The Poison King: The Life and Legend of Mithradates, Rome's Deadliest Enemy*. Princeton, NJ: Princeton UP, 2009.

## BOOKS FOR YOUNGER READERS

### Ancient Cultures

Hinds, Kathryn. *Scythians and Sarmatians*. New York: Marshall Cavendish Benchmark, 2010. Part of the *Barbarians!* series, a great introduction to Scythians and Sarmatians.

Napoli, Donna Jo, and Christina Balit. *Treasury of Greek Mythology: Classic Stories of Gods, Goddesses, Heroes & Monsters*. Washington, D.C.: National Geographic Society, 2011. Wonderful introduction to ancient Greek mythology and its links to real-life events, people, and places.

### Biographies

Bausum, Ann. *Dragon Bones and Dinosaur Eggs: A Photobiography of Roy Chapman Andrews*. Washington, D.C.: National Geographic Society, 2000. Photographic journey through the life of famed paleontologist Roy Chapman Andrews.

Marrin, Albert. *Secrets from the Rocks: Dinosaur Hunting with Roy Chapman Andrews*. New York: Dutton Children's, 2002. Biography of paleontologist Roy Chapman Andrews.

### Dinosaur Discoveries

Floca, Brian. *Dinosaurs at the Ends of the Earth: The Story of the Central Asiatic Expeditions*. New York: DK Ink, 2000. A mystery, a sandstorm, and dinosaurs in a fictional evocation of true events.

Halls, Kelly Milner, and Rick Spears. *Dinosaur Mummies: Beyond Bare-Bone Fossils*. Plain City, OH: Darby Creek Pub., 2003. Explores dinosaur mummies with discussion of fossilized soft tissue and internal organs.

Larson, Peter L., and Kristin Donnan. *Bones Rock!: Everything You Need to Know to Become a Paleontologist*. Montpelier, VT: Invisible Cities, 2004. Learn the skills needed to be a paleontologist plus information about summer dig opportunities.

### Monster Mania

Delano, Marfé Ferguson. *Sea Monsters: A Prehistoric Adventure*. Washington, D.C.: National Geographic Society, 2007. Pop-up book with 3-D computer-generated images of prehistoric sea monsters.

Keenan, Sheila. *Gods, Goddesses, and Monsters: A Book of World Mythology*. New York: Scholastic Reference, 2003. Introduction to myths from Asia to Africa to North and South America, with brief descriptions of the cast of characters.

Weber, Belinda. *Fabulous and Monstrous Beasts*. New York: Kingfisher, 2008. Background information on mythological monsters and fantastical beasts, with outstanding illustrations.

## ONLINE RESOURCES

### Podcasts featuring interviews with Adrienne

Interview from "Let's Talk Bigfoot!" on *Podbay*, March 19, 2009
podbay.fm/show/257243172/e/1237428889

Interview from "HNN #16: Geomythology, Rational Rap & Mr. Deity" on *The Humanist Hour*, February 28, 2007
podcast.thehumanist.org/2007/02/hnn-16-geomythology-rational-rap-mr-deity/

### Web pages about Adrienne and her work at Stanford University

Adrienne Mayor—Academic Papers
stanford.academia.edu/AdrienneMayor/Papers

Dinosaurs in Mythology
humanexperience.stanford.edu/feature-dragons

### Museum websites about dinosaurs and griffins

Dinosphere—The Children's Museum of Indianapolis
www.childrensmuseum.org/dinosphere/home

Griffin Bones—American Museum of Natural History
www.amnh.org/exhibitions/past-exhibitions/mythic-creatures/land-creatures-of-the-earth/griffin-bones

### A fun website about history that Adrienne contributes to

Wonders & Marvels
www.wondersandmarvels.com

# GLOSSARY/INDEX

# MY PART IN THIS BOOK

### By Marc Aronson

The making of this book is itself the crossing point of many stories and ways of telling stories. I first learned about Adrienne and her research on the auspicious day of July 4, 2000, when the *New York Times* published an article about her work called "Greek Myths Not Necessarily Mythical." The article itself was prompted by the recent publication of her book *The First Fossil Hunters* (Princeton University Press, 2000). So, the daily paper alerted me to a book published by a university press. Five years later, when her second fossil book, *Fossil Legends of the First Americans* (Princeton University Press, 2005), came out, I read both books and realized I had to speak with her. I found her email and asked her if she might want to work on a book for younger readers. I was thrilled that she not only liked the idea but had been thinking about that herself. We were both busy, but we began exchanging ideas. Then, in the summer of 2007, the American Museum of Natural History in New York City opened a show called "Mythic Creatures," and that gave us a chance to meet in person.

Adrienne had been deeply involved in the show, and she was my guide as we walked through it and then explored the dinosaur halls. Sitting outside in Central Park on a beautiful May day we sketched out what our book could be. I wrote up some ideas, sent them to her, but kept feeling there was more. So, I flew out to her home in Palo Alto, California, and sat there with a tape recorder and video camera and collected the story you have here.

Here is the adventure: from article, to book, to email, to conversation, to museum, to tape and film. What has woven all of this together is Adrienne's remarkable personality. She is steady, levelheaded, unflappable, and endlessly curious. That is the person I tried to capture: the quiet girl on the prairie; the dogged researcher who trusted her instincts and followed leads across hundreds of books and thousands of miles; the fresh-eyed scholar who found the nearly invisible trail left by our ancestors; the shy but firm voice of the outsider who knew, as sure as she knew the sky and earth of her childhood, that our forefathers and foremothers were observant, intelligent, and as curious as she is about the strange and wondrous bones and skeletons that peek out of the soil. I hope we all get to go exploring with her again soon—following along as she searches for wonders.